NOW THAT YOU HAVE THE KEYS:

Surviving Your First Year As Principal

CEMOND ROBINZINE, Ed. D.

The Robinzine Group, LLC
P.O. Box 81591
Conyers, Georgia, 30094
www.therobinzinegroup.com

Limits of Liability and Disclaimer of Warranty
The author and publisher shall not be liable for your misuse of this material. This book is strictly for informational and educational purposes.

Warning – Disclaimer
The purpose of this book is to educate and entertain. The author and/or publisher do not guarantee that anyone following these techniques, suggestions, tips, ideas, or strategies will become successful. The author and/or publisher shall have neither liability nor responsibility to anyone with respect to any loss or damage caused, or alleged to be caused, directly or indirectly by the information contained in this book.

***

Editing, Formatting and Cover Design done by Redfox Book Design

To my mother, Patricia Robinzine.

TABLE OF CONTENTS

INTRODUCTION

I would like to take this time to thank my Lord and Savior Jesus Christ for putting this project in my heart and all the opportunities He has afforded me throughout my career. A special thank you to my wife who is my rock and number one supporter! Thanks also to my kids who have lived this school administrator life with me for many years and finally, to my mom, who served as my first teacher and a teacher of many after serving over twenty years in the classroom. Thank God for obedience and His messenger!

I have over twenty years of experience in the field of education. I come from a family of educators. My mom, great-grandmother, aunts, and cousins have all served their communities as educators. My career started in the late nineties as a special educator in an elementary school in Lithonia, GA. I served as a special educator on the elementary, middle, and high school level. I began my career as a school administrator in 2007 and my tenure as a principal in 2014. During my first year as a principal my staff and I achieved great academic results for students! This included improving student achievement in the building significantly, especially math performance with our fifth-grade students, and maintaining retention rates at or above 90% during my tenure.

This book is written with the intent to prepare new principals for their journey. It can also serve as a refresher or reminder for veterans. I believe being a principal is one of the most rewarding careers an individual can achieve. The job will make you laugh, cry, challenge the status quo, and push yourself like you have never been pushed before to better the lives of the young people who have been put under your watch! Congratulations principal! Now the journey begins. Now that you have the keys to the building, how will you impact communities, build leaders under your supervision, improve teacher capacity, and most importantly equip learners with the knowledge and skills they need to go out into the world and compete in a global economy? Let's get started!!!

Welcome to your new position! The role of principal is one of the most important jobs in education, second only to classroom teachers. In this book, you will find key components that will help you survive your first year and become skilled at your position for years to come.

***

CHAPTER ONE
No Judgment!

Over the years as a principal supervisor, I have seen several new principals come into their new building and inspect the outgoing principal's work instead of evaluating the new work ahead. We will investigate the evaluation process and the power of evaluation in the later chapters. Right now, let's begin to look at what your first few days in your new position will look like.

Once you are approved as a new principal your tenure begins. Quite frequently, new principals spend a lot of time transitioning from their current assistant principal position into their full-time principal position. Let's take a deeper look into this. What I mean here is that the newly named principal begins to think more about what they must do to close out the assistant principal position instead of looking forward to what awaits them in their new building. Make sure, new principal, that your transition to your new building is no longer than a week or week and a half, if possible. You are now the leader of your own building and there are assignments and tasks that await you. Depending on the time of year that you are hired the need for you to get into your new building may be even more urgent. If you are hired mid-year the building should hopefully be functional, but if you are hired in the summer, time is of the essence. You will need to see if there are positions you need to fill, scheduling to complete, or classroom rosters to create; these are just a few items that may need your attention.

The first day is here and you arrive at your new building and receive your keys and hopefully have an opportunity to sit down with the outgoing principal. What notes will you take, questions will you ask, and what is around the corner that you should be informed about? Please remember, keep an open mind, and don't judge! Day two arrives and you are alone in the building for the first time. Have you reviewed arrival and dismissal procedures, scheduled meetings with your admin team, key stakeholders, and had time to review the school's current academic data?

You are beginning to form an opinion about your new school after meeting with your admin team and some stakeholders. What thoughts do you begin to formulate? Perhaps the following goes through your mind:

- *This school doesn't have certain structures like my old school*
- *The AP isn't as instructionally sound as I was as an AP*
- *The former principal only focused on climate and culture*
- *Teachers do whatever they want in this building*
- *My API has trouble creating a master schedule*
- *I want to wait but there are some things I must change now*
- *My athletic program needs new coaches*

If any of these things crossed your mind, let me remind you that you are in a no-judgment zone. Also, please keep in mind that you may be replacing a beloved leader, and don't feel as if you have to follow their blueprint. It is tougher sometimes to follow a beloved leader. Be patient because there is enough space for your talent, and you will be able to leave a positive legacy like your predecessor. Make sure you maintain your leadership style and lead from your place of comfort and strength. Observation without judgment during your first couple of weeks could really benefit you as you learn the job. Also, you have to keep in mind that for the first couple of weeks you are still learning your new role and the responsibilities that come with it. Give yourself time to learn the job. This will make your transition easier and assist you in managing any change processes within your new building. You are not an expert principal yet but continue to lead with your feet firmly planted in observation mode. Hopefully, you have been assigned a mentor at this point. I hope that your mentor will reinforce the idea about observing more and practicing leadership restraint with you for the first couple of months. Your relationship with your mentor will be "Mission Critical!" The value of a quality mentor for a new principal is priceless! The wisdom and experience they are able to offer you will be instrumental in your development into a successful principal. There are situations that you will need to receive guidance on and sometimes you won't want to ask your supervisor everything. A positive mentor/mentee relationship is long lasting. This relationship helps to mold and guide you into a successful school leader.

Make tough decisions in the beginning and seek counsel from your mentor or supervisor.

Also, be vulnerable and accept what you don't know. The principal's role is not like the assistant principal role. You are responsible for a lot more and you must make a lot of critical decisions in a short time. Please be reminded: don't judge or blame the previous principal for what is not right in YOUR current building. Once you are named principal you begin to take ownership for everything in that building. Make sure that you are viewing your new building through the right lens. The school is yours now and you have to own everything within those walls. You are not a consultant who comes in and evaluates the building and gives suggestions. So go ahead, embrace your new challenge, and get to work! Please! Please! In seeking assistance, don't express negative opinions about your staff and the school to others outside the building. This will only be perceived as ineptness by you and cast a blight on your skill set. Don't judge or blame the previous principal for what is not right in YOUR current building. Once you are named principal you begin to take ownership for everything in that building. Once you adopt this mentality the work can really begin, because you now have entered the "No Judgment Zone" and you are assuming the role of a new principal. Many times, I have observed that new principals apply for buildings that have traditionally underperformed. I have come to the conclusion that they apply for these buildings because they believe the former principal wasn't skilled; be careful not to fall into the place of judgment. Buildings that have traditionally underperformed can be a challenge for a new principal who isn't well-versed or familiar with school improvement in a very challenging setting. Being a principal and turning a building around is hard work and the first assignment in your new position is to not be judgmental. "Leadership is a selfless act of serving others more than others serving you."

***

NOTES

CHAPTER TWO
What's my plan?

I communicated a plan (90-day) during my interview and now is the time to begin implementing your plan. Let's begin by reviewing the plan before implementation to make sure it still fits the school's needs. If not, you may need to make a few adjustments to ensure your entry plan is suited to accomplish the goals you have created for your first ninety days; however, don't abandon the whole plan and begin becoming reactionary or fall into the practice of constantly putting out fires, due to the lack of systems within your building, specifically when responding to problems and concerns brought to you by teachers, parents, and other stakeholders. If you begin to lead in this fashion, you may not achieve the goals you have created. If you haven't created an entry plan it would be beneficial for you to sit down and create one. This plan will serve as a compass or North Star for you as you begin your new journey as a principal. Understanding change theory would really benefit you at this point of entry into your new position. The work will become difficult as the days go by but don't worry, remain consistent and stick to your plan. Please keep in mind that you won't see progress every day; however, if you remain consistent, progress will come. Consistent monitoring will alert you of progress being made or to any adjustments to your plan that your leadership team may need to make. Progress may be made incrementally, but that is okay! When you are making progress make sure that you acknowledge it and begin to build on that momentum with your staff. As a new principal you must know what making progress looks like and how close you are to accomplishing your vision, at all times. Do:

- *Spend your first days, weeks, and months wisely (building relationships, examining processes, holding back from making significant changes)*
- *Make sure your plan is research based and your ideas are current*
- *Own your plan and personalize it*
- *Make sure your leadership actions are observed as being consistent by your faculty and staff*
- *Ensure that your communication about your plan is clear and concise to your faculty and staff; clear, concise, and timely communication will be well received by your staff. This helps them meet your expectations.*

***

NOTES

CHAPTER THREE
Stick to your plan!

Now is not the time to change course from what you originally put into your plan. You are now in the position, and it looks different from your view now versus when you were an assistant principal or in your previous position. It seems as if someone has pulled back the curtains and offered you a backstage pass to your favorite artist's concert. You didn't realize so much went on behind the scenes. That is the reason why sticking to your entry plan is so critical. Your entry plan will serve as a road map upon which to build a solid foundation; by reviewing your current budget, schedules, IEP's, vacancies in the building, operational systems, and forming positive relationships within your building with all stakeholders, it will allow you to pivot into making positive changes in the building in the future if needed.

You have been in your new role for a few months now and believe a few things are going to have to change if you want to achieve the goals created in your plan. Before making your changes ask yourself a couple of questions:

- *Is it imperative that I make the change now?*
- *Who all will be impacted by this change?*
- *Who do I need in the building to assist me with the change?*
- *Will the change have an immediate positive impact on student achievement?*

- *Are there ethical implications if I don't act now?*

For instance, there are some issues I have discovered while in my new position that need to be addressed immediately due to unethical behavior before my appointment. Let's discuss this type of situation. This isn't a judgment of the previous admin team; this is something concrete that needs to be handled because it is in violation of district policy. For instance, the financial records are disordered, or IEPs aren't up to date. These types of issues need to be addressed immediately.

A good principal always knows that one decision or change has a domino effect within the building. Whenever a decision is made within your building, always look at how the dominos will fall; the decisions you make as a principal don't only impact you, but others are impacted as well. For instance, a change in arrival time impacts parents, teachers, and students. Parents may have to change care for students, teachers may have students who attend the school as well, and student attendance could be impacted negatively which impacts student achievement. When you do make changes remember to always monitor, monitor, and monitor whatever process you have changed to make sure it is working to achieve your desired outcomes. Refer to chapter 1, and don't be evaluative. The building is yours now and you have to own everything in it. There will be times when you will have to make changes in the building and some of your employees may not be happy with the changes you make. For instance, you may review the data for your new building and realize that in a certain content area, students performed really low on a certain grade level. Based on this data you may have to move some teachers out of their comfort zone and place them on a grade level they aren't familiar with. If you have to make this type of adjustment don't be afraid to make changes you believe will have a positive impact on student achievement. Also, at this point you may begin to receive criticism from staff members in the building or outside individuals because of some of the changes that may be coming. Please don't take the criticism personally. All good principals have received some level of criticism. Once you gain the ability to let the criticism roll off your back you will be on your way to maturing in your new position. I know, I know it doesn't feel good to be talked about in a negative fashion but remember to maintain your focus and you will gain more supporters than critics.

"YOU'VE GOT THIS!"

***

NOTES

CHAPTER FOUR
Rhythm and Pace

A principal's day is very busy! From checking emails, attending parent meetings, meting out discipline, to completing reports etc., every second of the day counts for a principal whether you are new or a veteran. A principal must be able to pivot consistently throughout the day. You don't want to spend so much time on one item that you begin to neglect other areas of the job. For instance, you don't want to spend too much time on disciplinary issues. Rather, you would benefit from creating a system to investigate disciplinary issues where you gather the facts and come to a conclusion in a timely fashion. Keep in mind that your primary responsibility is to be an instructional leader. If you end up majoring in the minor, you may begin to lose your focus and classroom instruction can end up taking a backseat. Where you spend most of your time will impact your building the most in a positive or negative fashion. Also, rhythm and pace can be impacted if you haven't evaluated your strengths and weaknesses, meaning that many leaders find themselves spending the majority of their workday on tasks only that they enjoy or are comfortable with. Make sure that you spend time developing your skill set so that you are well rounded and know every aspect of running your new building. This is where the relationship with your coach is so valuable. Being able to receive quality feedback and constructive criticism with regards to your growth areas is needed for your development.

To help you maximize your day you should create a daily schedule and try to stick to it as closely as possible. Using a scheduler or assigning your secretary the duty of scheduler will assist you with this. For example, if you plan on observing classes on Monday from 8:00 -10:00, let your admin team and secretary know not to interrupt, short of an emergency during this time. This may sound simple, but it isn't if you haven't worked on prioritizing your day. Too many leaders fall into the habit of putting out fires, instead of growing their instructional program due to a lack of systems in their buildings. My old principal used to say *"You need to know your job, the man below you, and the man above you. Find your workflow and begin to lead from that place."*

***

NOTES

CHAPTER FIVE
Delegation/Evaluation

What are my team's strengths and weaknesses? When you enter a new building, you will need to evaluate your team's strengths and weaknesses and how their skill set connects to your vision for the school. Keep in mind we are not judging but assessing skill sets to see how they connect to your new vision.

Assign your team roles and responsibilities (make sure you are clear and concise about your admin team's duties). Assign roles and duties to your admin staff also; for example, who will answer the phones and how you want the calls managed, a lunch schedule, break and summer schedule, etc. This is very important as a lot of planning takes place over the summer and you need people in the building to register students. Who will create duty rosters, schedules, class lists, and send communication out to parents? How will the evaluation schedule be scheduled? Will you only evaluate new teachers or allow your AP's to participate in their evaluation? (I have attached a sample evaluation schedule for you to review). Who will own the school's calendar? Who will reconcile the financials every month? Who will manage the PLC's, leadership team meetings, admin meetings, and collaborative planning meetings? Building teacher capacity is important.

Scheduling; are you meeting with your admin team daily and weekly? Who is on your team?

This is one of the most important roles of a new principal. You have observed processes in the building for a few months and now you are ready to begin evaluating systems. The operative word here is systems. Program and systems evaluation is often overlooked by principals; however, if more time was spent evaluating systems and programs by principals, they could become more efficient in the school improvement process. As a new principal you need to create a list of all the programs used in your building i.e., educational software, literacy/math resources, and remediation programs to name a few. Once you have created the list, review the program's effectiveness and connection to your current school improvement plan and make the necessary adjustments as needed. This information will assist you in managing the process in your building. In some cases, there may be a lack of systems in your new building. That is alright, it only presents an opportunity for you to create the appropriate system in your building to fill the void. Make sure when you implement a new system that it is connected to your continuous improvement plan which should lead to increased student learning outcomes. Remember that you are principal and the individuals assigned to you are there to support you. Be mindful that your admin teams need to grow, but ultimately, they are there to support the principal's vision.

Administrative Responsibilities Chart

Principal	Admin 1	Admin 2
AM/PM Bus Duty	Testing	Duty Assignments (Staff)
Announcements	Scheduling	AM Cafeteria/PM Bus Duty or Hall Duty
Assembly Approval	Car Rider Duty AM/PM	Faculty Attendance/Student Attendance (Affidavits/POR)
Field Trip Requests	Retention Meetings	504's
School Council	Discipline	Discipline
Fire & Disaster Drills	Instructional Supplies	Lunch Duty
Partners in Education	Lunch Duty	Staff Evaluations
Special Education/Title One	Lesson Plans/E.R. included	Event Supervision
Budget	MTSS	Facilities
FTE Counts	Staff Evaluations	Staff Duty Roster
Facilities	Event Supervision	
Event Supervision	Keys	
TOTY/CPOTY	SIEP	
Leave Requests	Facilities	
Staff Evaluations		
Event Supervision		
Testing includes: GKIDS, CFA's, Georgia Milestones, and any other school or district assessments		
Regular School Hours 7 am – 4 pm		

"A growth mindset is contagious."

NOTES

CHAPTER SIX
Performance Management

In this chapter we will discuss how to manage personnel who may be experiencing performance issues. Always remember that as a leader you want to make sure that your employees have the opportunity to grow and that your expectations are very clear. When faced with an employee who is exhibiting performance issues ask yourself is this a "skill or will " issue? To ensure this is not a skill issue you should coach your employee around the deficient area you have observed and make sure that your expectations and feedback are clear. Essential to this process is that you and your leadership team are very consistent in your communication and that feedback is aligned to ensure that your employee is given every opportunity to grow and meet your expectations. If your employee is not responding to your coaching and feedback cycles, it may be time to begin redirecting. A lot of new and old administrators struggle with holding employees accountable. In my years of experience this is the area most administrators need coaching in. Keep in mind that achievement in your building is only as good as the lowest performing educator in your building. Accountability will be discussed further in one of the later chapters. Effective communication is part of performance management. Effective communication is an invaluable skill set for any good administrator. Communication is the glue to perfect execution of expectations. Principals must communicate over and over their goals and expectations to their stakeholders, both internal and external. When dealing with staff or personnel that are not meeting district or building level expectations, the principal must ensure that effective communication is on-going. Communication and explicit documentation is a must.

***

NOTES

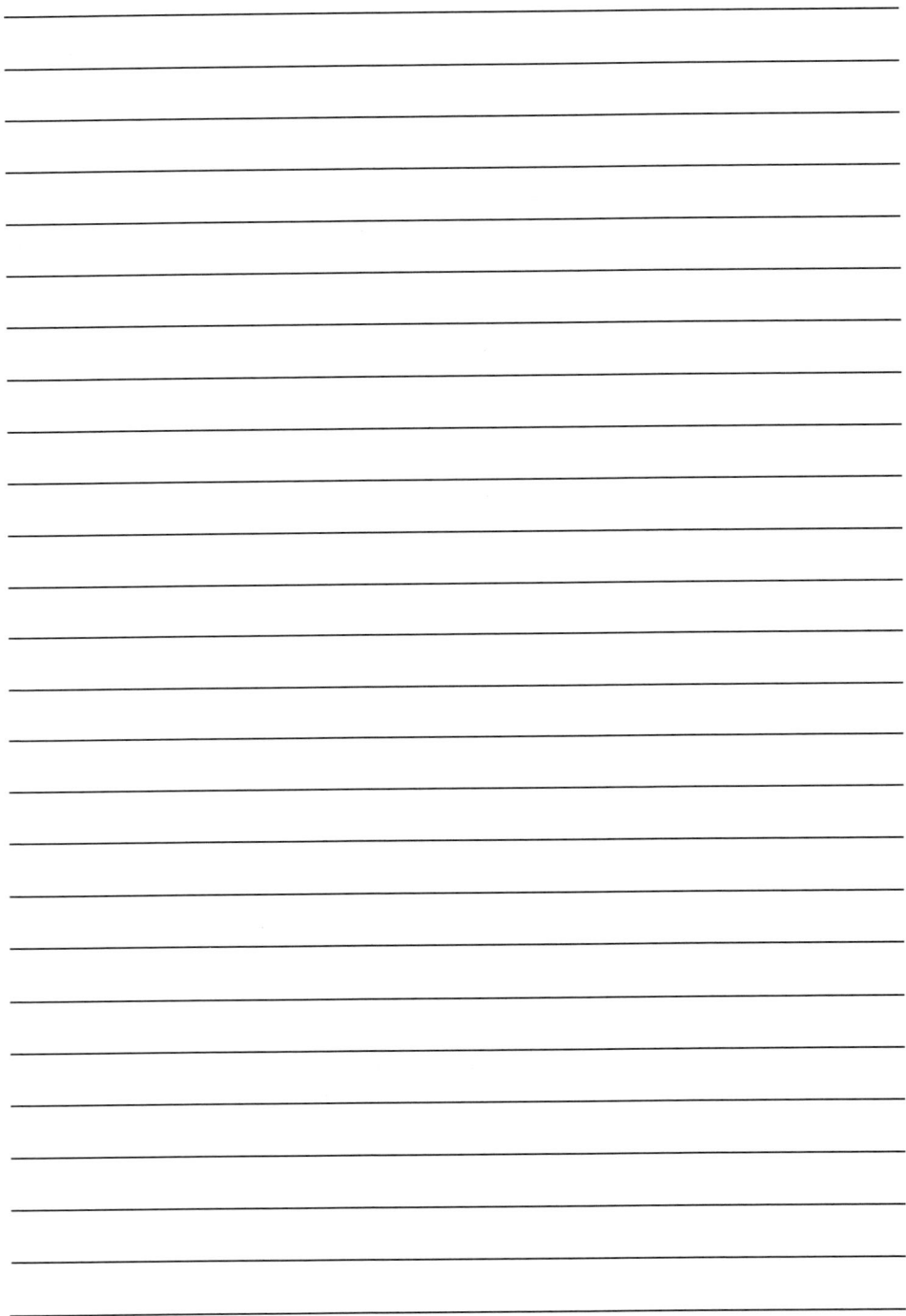

CHAPTER SEVEN
Celebrations

Celebrating success in a new building no matter how large or small helps to build a positive school culture. Make time to highlight the positive in your building and not focus on all the things you perceive to be negative or not going right at this point. Take time to get to know something about each one of your teachers personally. Also, begin to study your staff's individual strengths and weaknesses. No gain or victory in your first couple of months is too small to celebrate. If staff attendance increases, formative data results are trending up, or parent complaints are down. Take time in a faculty meeting to highlight the positive things that are going on in your new building.

Branding the school and telling your story is a very important step that should not be overlooked. You are now in the building and need to tell a very positive story about your building and begin the branding process. Remember, whatever you put out in the community will stick. Refer to chapter 1, and don't be evaluative. The building is yours now and this is the time where you begin to create a culture of winning and rebranding your building. Please don't minimize this step. Rebranding your building is crucial because you are the face of the school.

Your voice and walk are important. The principal position places you front and center before your staff and all stakeholders. Be prepared because your staff members, especially the front office, will monitor your every move. This is not a bad thing, they want to make sure they are meeting your expectations, so be very clear when setting expectations for your office staff.

People watch your every step as a principal. This takes a little time to get used to. It is imperative that you model your expectations. If you want the staff to be on time, you need to arrive on time, everything you expect from them you must model in your administrative walk. Also, don't take the criticism personally. I believe this is one of the biggest challenges for a new principal to accept; being talked about or criticized by staff, parents, or other stakeholders. The criticism will come but as long as you stay focused on the vision and know that you are making decisions in the best interest of the students, you will be fine.

Write your story and guide the narrative. Celebrate victories with your team in an authentic fashion no matter how big or small. Your staff wants to please you and they need to hear from you when they have met your expectations. It would be beneficial to create some sort of monthly award or celebration that highlights the great work going on in your building. You and your staff members are on your way to improving student achievement like you have never seen before!

YOU'VE GOT THIS!

***

NOTES

CHAPTER EIGHT
Work/Life Balance and Self Care

This is one of the final chapters for a reason; not to minimize its value but to leave you with this final thought. The principal's job is very stressful and the demands on a principal grow each year. In my first year as a principal I was assigned to a mentor. My mentor was instrumental in my growth and development as a school administrator. After our first meeting she explained to me that she was going to give me some homework. I cringed at the thought of more homework, but my assignment would be one of the most valuable lessons I learned during my career. She said, "I want you to go home and not do any work, find something you enjoy doing and do it!" That assignment has always resonated with me, and I continue to task my leaders with that assignment. It is very hard to lead when you are married to the job and don't take time to unplug, rest, and rejuvenate yourself. You are making tough decisions daily that can challenge relationships in the building and sometimes you can't really control the outcomes of some of the decisions you have to make. This is very difficult for others outside of the position to understand. I would strongly encourage you to find an outlet outside of your job to really help you unwind and become rejuvenated. This could mean going home on time at least once a week to enjoy something you like outside of your job. Maintaining a good work/life balance is essential in the life of a principal, in my opinion. You need to be balanced emotionally and physically to sustain the demands placed on you on a year-to-year basis. Maintaining or obtaining a hobby outside of work can help you maintain that balance. Also, bring your identity to the job and don't let the job become your identity. What I mean here is be the authentic you and the person the committee hired to do the job. Your beliefs and approach to the job will be challenged from time to time due to bureaucracy, leadership changes, and simply because of the huge expectations placed on your shoulders. With that being said, don't be afraid to lead! Leading is lonely and you have to be courageous to lead! So, lead your staff, students, and community courageously! Leading courageously means there will be times in your position that you will have to make decisions that make you uncomfortable. Always make the decisions by putting students first and connecting your decision to the school's vision and you will never go wrong!

Stay current and remain flexible! This means that you are up to date on the current literature and best practices to make you an efficient leader. Flexibility means remaining open to change and constructive criticism and feedback from your supervisor and mentors. This is critical to your development and growth. Also, self-care is very important so please don't minimize this aspect of your life. This portion is valuable because the job of a new principal can become overwhelming and stressful if you don't take time to unplug and refresh. The decisions you have to make and the demands on your schedule can be physically and emotionally draining. I would like to encourage you to find an outlet and make time on your calendar at least once a week to engage in something you enjoy outside of work.

YOU'VE GOT THIS!

It is good to have a principal buddy or a partner in the work environment. This individual is someone you can call to ask questions, or they call you to remind you of things that need to be turned in. Also, this individual can be that listening ear that you so desperately need at times. You will be challenged physically and emotionally whilst in the seat. During your challenging times is when your leadership will be most on display. I would advise you to remain authentic and lead courageously. Your staff and students will benefit greatly from your consistent, authentic, and courageous leadership. Courageous leadership entails making tough decisions for staff and students, saying what you mean and meaning what you say, and being committed to your community and the school's vision. It also includes leading with integrity and understanding that you are a leader of people, and your impact will be felt beyond your tenure.

You were hired in this position for a reason, and you should step up and lead boldly. Don't lose your passion or creativity during your tenure because of bureaucracy, difficult parents, slow progress, fierce conversations, etc. Keep fighting for your school and your community!

***

NOTES

CHAPTER NINE
You've Got This!

The role of today's principal is demanding and challenging. It is also one of the most rewarding jobs in education, in my opinion, especially when you lead from a place that is all about students and affording them the best education possible whilst in your care. You were selected to be in your role for a reason. Someone saw something special in you so go forward and make your school and community better for the young lives that are in your care daily. You are leading in unprecedented times and your wellness should be high on the priority list. A new leader once asked me, "What is one piece of advice you would offer a new principal?" I responded with "Visualize how you want to finish." This type of thinking can assist you with creating the steps needed to achieve your goal.

Don't worry,

YOU'VE GOT THIS!!!

***

NOTES

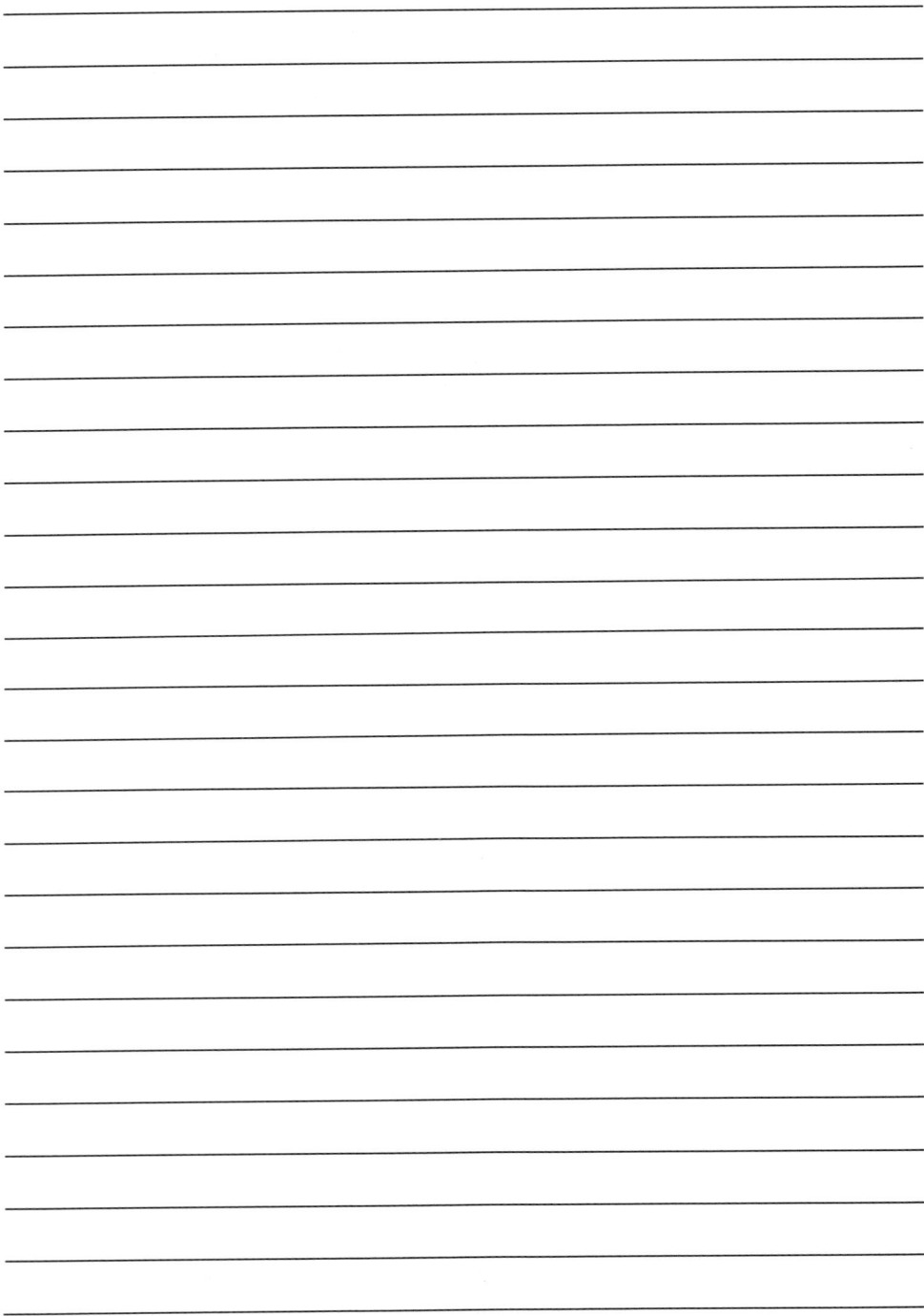

CHAPTER TEN
Courageous Leadership

As a leader you will be faced with numerous decisions to make, and some will be difficult. I challenge you to be courageous enough to make the right decisions for your students and your community. Now more than ever, leaders, especially educational leaders are being challenged in ways they have never been challenged before. Budding leaders must be able to face these challenges with an open mindset and a commitment to remain flexible during these uncertain times. Many new leaders are leading buildings with little to no experience under their belts. Make the most of your opportunity and use this time to be creative and intentional about the organizational design and culture you will create for your staff and students. Being intentional about how your building is designed and the culture you create will dictate learning outcomes for students. Remember, being courageous doesn't mean you want to face challenges, but being decisive sends the right message to your staff and community. Kicking the can or playing the middle is a bad decision. When you are faced with making tough decisions, gather all the facts you need to make an informed decision. Also, you don't have to be super quick to respond; quick responses can sometimes be reactive and lead to problems in the future. Be slow to react and quick to gather all the facts!! Move closer to achieving your school's goals and be courageous because your school community needs you to be!!

NOTES

CHAPTER ELEVEN
Don't stop until you get knocked out!

This chapter is near and dear to me because of the message behind it. I am an African American male who grew up in suburban Atlanta. Statistics say I shouldn't have made it as far as I have. I am standing on the shoulders of giants and greatness. My great-grandfather migrated from Marks, Mississippi to Atlanta, Ga. Please keep in mind that Marks was titled one of the poorest cities in the nation by Dr. King during the Poor People's Movement. Also, my great-grandmother was a college graduate from Albany State. I am standing on the shoulders of giants and my relatives before me would not stop fighting until they were able to make a better way for the future. I feel an obligation to keep fighting for our children who have been underserved, villainized, and marginalized. I have committed myself to not stop fighting for what is right until I can't fight anymore.

The title for this chapter came to me while serving as an assistant superintendent. I would joke with my secretary from time to time using different slogans and this one happened to stick. This is the type of action and energy our leaders need to possess to create the type of schools our students need and deserve. Relentless passion fueled by hope that our schools will one day serve in the capacity they were created to serve in. We want to see young ALL young learners reading on grade level by third grade, fewer kids of color referred to special education, more authentic learning experiences for students, financial literacy taught at a young age, less sit and get, and more civic instruction to help our students begin to understand their role in building up their own communities. This type of work calls for authentic leaders who aren't afraid to challenge the status quo and who are committed to selflessness. This type of leadership isn't easy, but it embodies the right actions for our students.

Education was built around an agrarian calendar and hasn't been truly amended since its inception. Leading through Covid-19 has truly presented educators with the opportunity to amend a system that has not reached all students historically. We have a great opportunity to amend the learning environment for students to meet all their needs. To build this type of learning environment we need principals who aren't afraid to advocate for equity for all students. This means being able to articulate factual evidence to school leaders to promote positive change in our classrooms. Our students need school leaders who won't stop advocating for their educational needs! Schools need leaders who will not remain silent amidst layers of bureaucracy. Leaders, our students need you to carry out what you committed to when you visualized becoming the leader of the building you now serve in! Please school leaders, don't stop fighting for students until you get knocked out!

***

NOTES

CHAPTER TWELVE
Accountability vs. Tyranny

Education has changed tremendously over the last three to five years. Constant initiative changes, Covid-19, employee shortages, etc. What has led us to this point and where will we land? With so many changes taking flight in education we have adopted a definition of accountability that has led to a massive exodus of professionals out of teaching. Accountability is ensuring everyone is working in your building to better the lives of the students they serve. Tyranny is sending a bunch of documents and checklists to leaders and teachers to complete that have no impact on learning, improving teaching, or leader development. Leadership and compliance are not synonymous. This type of compliance driven leadership has contributed majorly to the mass exodus of teachers. Accountability begins with a leader. All good school leaders typically hold themselves to high standards and model their expectations through their daily walk.

When accountability begins with the leader, the impact on your staff is greater. Self-accountability limits the finger pointing and blame game that happens a lot in our schools and has no impact on improving student achievement.

***

NOTES

CHAPTER THIRTEEN
Your Legacy!

After September 11, 2001, the CEO of FEDEX was quoted as stating that "Leaders in times of crisis must embrace the current reality and give people a sense of hope." I agree totally with that statement. You are leading in unparalleled times and now more than ever your faculty and staff needs you to plant seeds of hope for them and your students. Don't avoid or escape the times that you are leading through. Take this time to create and design systems in your building that will catapult your school community to the next level. This could be a strong focus on identifying more gifted students in your building and exiting more students out of remedial programs that they have been placed in. Schools have traditionally remediated more students than they have accelerated. Hope for your community doesn't happen by chance, be intentional about your actions and let your hope for a strong school community be the driving force behind your intentionality.

Will you be credible? What will the leaders under you go on to do or become? Your legacy begins upon your arrival in the building for the first time. Don't assume you have years to get the building where you want it to be. Time flies in the principal's seat, so make sure that you make every day count. Great leaders influence others to do great things and leave a lasting impact on the staff and students they come in contact with on a daily basis. Be the leader who leaves a positive impact on others by never forgetting that relationships matter, your actions and how you treat people are a part of your legacy. Lead your way and leave a positive long-standing legacy!!! Please use the journal pages to jot down the legacy you envision leaving. I wish you the best on this journey!

***

NOTES

ABOUT THE AUTHOR

Dr. Cemond T. Robinzine grew up in East Point, Georgia, and brings over two decades of invaluable experience in the field of education. His journey has spanned across various educational levels, including elementary, middle, and high school, contributing significantly to the development and growth of students, as well as adult.

Dr. Robinzine has worn multiple hats throughout his illustrious career, serving in roles such as a dedicated teacher, insightful assistant principal, diligent school improvement specialist, and astute assistant superintendent within the public education system. His diverse roles have not only shaped his understanding of education from various perspectives but have also allowed him to play a pivotal role in enhancing the educational landscape.

Raised in a family with a rich legacy of educators, Dr. Robinzine draws inspiration from his roots. A long line of educators in his family instilled in him a profound love for learning and a deep-seated commitment to serving the community. These values have become the driving force behind his career, motivating him to create positive and impactful changes within the realm of education.

In addition to his professional accomplishments, Dr. Robinzine is a passionate advocate for fostering a love of learning, educational equity, and community engagement. His dedication to these principles shines through in both his professional endeavors and personal values, making him not just an educator but a beacon of inspiration for those who aspire to make a lasting impact in the world of education and beyond.

Dr. Robinzine is also a proud husband and father of three children. He enjoys his free time golfing with his friends, reading, and traveling around the globe.

Dr. Robinzine is a part of the Robinzine Group, LLC., the family's educational consultant company. The Robinzine Group, LLC., is ready to handle all of your educational needs. Please contact us at robinzine3@bellsouth.net or 404-468-8026.

ACKNOWLEDGEMENTS

During the journey of bringing this book to fruition, I am deeply indebted to those whose unwavering support and influence have been the pillars of my success.

My wife, Dr. Monique T. Robinzine: Your boundless motivation and unwavering support have been my rock. Words cannot adequately express my gratitude for your encouragement, patience, and belief in me. This book is as much yours as it is mine.

My mom, Patricia Robinzine: A dedicated teacher for over two decades, you have been a beacon of resilience, fighting against inequities and serving students in poverty with unmatched passion. Your commitment to education and your selfless dedication to making a difference have been a constant source of inspiration. This book is a tribute to your enduring legacy.

My father, Clarence E. Robinzine Jr.: Thank you for instilling in me a strong work ethic and an unyielding commitment to family. Your guidance and values have been the compass guiding me through life's journey. This book is a reflection of the principles you've imparted.

My high school principal, Dr. Herschel Robinson: An exemplar of leadership, service, and dedication, you set the standard for excellence in our school community. Your impact on my understanding of leadership is immeasurable, and I am grateful for the lessons learned under your guidance.

My college professor, Dr. Dianne Hammitt: Your belief in me and support during the formative years of my education provided the foundation for my academic and professional pursuits. Your mentorship has been instrumental in shaping my path, and I am thankful for your unwavering encouragement.

To all those mentioned above, and to countless others who have contributed to this journey in various ways, I extend my deepest appreciation. This book is a reflection of the collective support and inspiration that has fueled its creation.

Thank you!